The Revelation of
The Book of Zohar
in Our Time

Bnei Baruch
Kabbalah Education & Research Institute
Kabbalah.info

2

The Revelation of
The Book of Zohar
in Our Time

The Zohar Speaks to the Heart of Us All

Question: What's the significance of *The Book of Zohar* in Our Time? Are we now obligated to study *The Zohar* in order to attain spirituality?

Yes, it's clear cut. I've been waiting for that for a long time and I didn't want to start the study of *The Zohar* prematurely. I even said the contrary, "Why should we study *The Zohar*?" One might have assumed that Baal HaSulam composed the work of his life for no particular reason but, of course, that's incorrect. The idea is that we had to be prepared for it.

Today, we're beginning to study *The Book of Zohar* with everyone because we have become of a sufficient mass to attain a position allowing us to climb up the same ladder together. Whoever can nullify himself with all of his might like a baby, studying together with us out of the desire to enter the feeling discussed in *The Book of Zohar*, is welcome to join the study. This study doesn't require intellect and not many sketches can be drawn or learned throughout. *The Book of Zohar* speaks to the heart for the purpose of opening a person's emotions regarding the discernments of bestowal and receiving. Hence, Baal HaSulam entitled his commentary "The Ladder" rather than any other name.

The sections of *The Zohar* aren't equal. Some parts are simple in their language and depth and other parts are more difficult. We won't study in order of the weekly portions. Rather, we will begin with the simpler sections and going forward, it is similar to what we learn about the order of clarifications. When we have 'entered' emotionally, which is to say after we have become accustomed to *The Book of Zohar's* style and have focused ourselves properly, we will be prepared to study other sections as well. Then, we won't only yearn, we will actually crave for *The Zohar*, we will develop a sort of particular appetite for it. The truth is that there is no difference between the depths of each and every section of *The Zohar*. Rashbi and Baal HaSulam interpreted them to their fullest spiritual degree. The difference is only with reference to us who are the students.

Excerpt from the daily Kabbalah lesson, Nov. 19, 2009

It's Time

Question: What's so special about this period compared to previous ones for us to now begin studying *The Book of Zohar*?

The difference is in the preparation. We spoke about unity and related issues at great length until we realized nothing would help us other than unity.

We have always said that it was impossible to read *The Book of Zohar* without a group but, now, we actually feel it "on our own flesh." I believe that couldn't have been reached previously. Even though we discussed it, we weren't yet willing to go and "cut the ego out of us" as, otherwise, we wouldn't attain anything. Previously, we didn't have the mindset to reach that internal decision.

I hope that today, with the help of the general effort and the help of the authors of *The Book of Zohar*, we will attain that. I don't think we had the opportunity to attain that prior to opening the television channel which elevated us to another degree of our internality.

Excerpt from the virtual lesson on *The Book of Zohar*, Nov. 15, 2009

The Zohar as the Means for Salvation

Question: Is there a group feeling of the Creator?

There is personal, individual attainment and there is group attainment. For now, we're at the stage of individual attainment and are attempting to shift into group attainment. That's the future of the world from our generation forward. The wisdom of Kabbalah has been specifically revealed today in order to lead the entire world to group attainment.

That's the reason we're now beginning to study *The Book of Zohar* which was composed by a group and is revealed only in a group. The primary issue is the mutual connection among people that resembles the connection among the members of Rabbi Shimon Bar Yochai's group who wrote this book.

As previously mentioned, the world stands before a

new era in which the revelation must be in a group. Actually, the whole world is one group. That's identical to the events near Mount Sinai. Hatred existed among people but they were told, "If you do not demand the Creator now, then here, with the hatred amongst you, shall be the place of your burial."

Despite the hatred, one condition was set before them which was to bond as one man with one heart. However, that's impossible as I hate everyone so much that I can't bear to look at them even if it costs me my life! Then, the Creator, the Upper Force, is revealed spreading peace between these two opposites. The spiritual vessel is the depth of the egoistic desire from below, the screen from above, and the Upper Light residing between them.

We have to reach the situation in which, on the one hand, we hate each other, on the other hand, we love each other, and yet we demand the revelation of the force of bestowal among us.

That's what stands before our generation. We're in the process of advancement toward global unity and that's why we're studying *The Book of Zohar*. We're prepared for it, undoubtedly. We hope the world will also reach the realization that such a possibility exists and that it will happen peacefully.

Excerpt from daily Kabbalah lesson December 4, 2009

The Book of Zohar Is Open to All

Question: What should be the internal work of a person watching the Internet or television during the reading of *The Zohar*?

The Book of Zohar is an opportunity for us all to reveal the true reality within us. A person who organizes and sorts out our current reality, along with revealing its internality, senses within not only this world but the spiritual world as well. Then, he doesn't encounter any conflict between the corporeal world seemingly outside of him and the spiritual world inside him or between the concealed and the revealed. Rather, everything is revealed within his desires. Correction of our desires allows us to open our ability to see them and to feel them.

It's important to stress that even people who aren't as prepared as we are to perceive *The Zohar* can join the studies and gain the exact same qualities. It's similar to a baby born today. The adults provide him with all of his needs based on what was prepared for them in previous generations and adapted to the level of today's world.

Thus, those "infants" joining us today who are our new members can merit the exact same revelations we expect and there is no difference between us. They will hear to the extent they are willing to hear, to the extent of their unity with us, and their annulment before the studies. When I hear that they are anxious and anticipating, and perhaps even reverent of this study, I am filled with joy because such a feeling is a vital condition for connecting with *The Book of Zohar*.

Excerpt from the daily Kabbalah lesson, December 7, 2009

Preparation for *Studying The Book of Zohar*

Preparation for studying *The Zohar* should be special and emotional. It should be a type of yearning like craving for a loved one. There are no words to describe it. This emotion should involve a little pain, a little desire, and a little love. It should be like a silent concern for the object of your desire, internal and constant, and a type of longing. It should be a preparation and not an assault. It shouldn't be crass or intellectual, but a true inner bonding.

Excerpt from a Kabbalah lesson, Nov 13, 2009

Constant Preparation for Studying *The Zohar*

The Zohar requires great preparation of us prior to its reading, while reading and following the reading, and actually, all the time. It elevates the individual to a certain degree from which he mustn't fall. From the moment he starts reading the book and onwards, his life begins to operate on two levels. On one level, he exists within the text of *The Zohar* and, simultaneously, on the level of "beast" as well. However, from the moment he is at the level of studying *The Zohar*, he never leaves it.

Hence, all the other scriptures we read should be an addition for discerning and providing additional tools to help us merge with this text. Everything, including in regular life and in our connection with friends, already constitutes an added contribution to perceive, to permeate, and to be familiar with this book.

Accordingly, each one should organize all of reality and his entire life.

I remember that when I began studying *The Book of Zohar*, it truly designated a type of change which was a dramatic change for me. The power of *The Zohar* is found in the way it stabilizes the individual and leads him to a certain steady state in which he remains all the time. *The Zohar* provides us with a certain spirit and height and then, everything we do becomes an addition which increases that height.

Excerpt from the daily Kabbalah lesson, December 4, 2009

The Condition for Opening *The Book of Zohar*

I think that studying about the "three lines" is the critical area where one should demand feeling. This is because working with the three lines is all-inclusive: restricting the desire to receive, elevating to *Binah*, merging with the Creator, receiving the force of bestowal from Him on top of one's original desire, and building the soul with 'receiving in order to bestow' along with the work of the "face." The three lines is the comprehensive usable formula for the creature within the will to receive from the beginning of our work until the end of correction.

While studying about the three lines, we should demand reactions and feelings resembling those we experience when engaged in internal struggles of life similar to cases in which we encounter an inner conflict such as when you must get up but can't, or when there is candy in front of you and you debate whether to eat it or not. If we turn that demand into a general prayer, it will surely happen.

Excerpt from the daily Kabbalah lesson, September 21, 2009

The Zohar Leads us to a
Transformed View of the World

We must be prepared for this as studying *The Zohar* leads us to a transformed view of the world, of our lives, and of everything taking place within and outside of us. *The Zohar* begins to focus us and to give us a different perspective from the one we've been used to up until now. We will begin to view the texts we read differently. Even when we sing our songs, we will see the roots which are the reasons for everything taking place around us. We will begin to sense how the spiritual world exists within the corporeal world and activates and revolves it.

Thus, gradually, we will gain some type of true feeling of the activating, protecting, bestowing and leading force which will be totally new discernments regarding the Creator. Therefore, we must try to remain inspired from the lesson as much as possible, to enter it to the greatest extent, and to live reality with a single desire.

The Creator created one desire and we exist within it. *The Book of Zohar* tells us about that desire and all that takes place within it. We would like to see, understand, feel, and to experience everything taking place within that entire desire called "reality". It's of extreme importance to continue that inspiration and that enlightenment as much as possible when we leave the lesson and not to let it be extinguished.

Excerpt from the daily Kabbalah lesson, November 22, 2009

The Approach to Studying
Studying
The Book of Zohar

Awakening Myself into Consciousness

Some people think *The Zohar* speaks of morals as if turning to us as a kindergarten teacher would to her children, saying, "You should be nice to each other." Others think that *The Zohar* tells us about the world or spiritual mysticism way "out there" disconnected from us. Some think that *The Zohar* tells us nothing but, rather, it constitutes a certain connection separate from us in a way understood only by Kabbalists. And then there are others who read it as a type of remedy for health or success in life.

There are numerous approaches and we're comprised of them all. We're in an ocean of preconceived notions regarding *The Book of Zohar* and we need to fight them. All of those notions exist within us and are influencing us through the public after thousands of years of viewing *The Zohar* this way. Hence, we need to constantly work on ourselves.

Out of all of those approaches, we choose the first and foremost one which is the perception of reality. In the meantime, we're not adding our internal work to it which is called the "work of the Creator." It's possible to add many discernments and further searching to the study since *The Zohar* tells us of a complete entity, of true reality, and the different discernments therein. However, we don't wish to do so.

When we start studying *The Book of Zohar*, we desire to establish the proper approach to the written word. I don't care what's written; I'll know that afterward when *The Zohar* opens to me, when the Surrounding Light that it brings influences me, when I begin to be inspired, and, to a certain extent, when I work with reality as it's revealed.

In the meantime, I must only direct myself the entire time, upholding myself, and maintaining my proper approach to the opening of the book. I don't open it mystically but I permeate the material itself. I open the book and I see my inner attributes which are only my desires and nothing else beyond that. My inner, spiritual anatomy is depicted before me. I don't open my biological body but my soul which is also made of those same parts as my body. In addition, it includes everything I see in the surrounding world as everything exists within the soul. Those are the parts I want to identify and to concentrate on now.

That's how we need to teach ourselves to relate to *The Zohar*. *The Zohar* speaks of the soul alone. The soul is the entire desire created by the Creator and I wish to discern all of its levels, attributes, and connections within.

So, let's continue to maintain this approach all the time. It can be compared to a baby who, before beginning to understand the world and respond to it, must first see that the world exists. That's why we play something for him or give him something shiny. We want it to enter his field of vision and sight. Likewise, for now, we only need to discern the qualities spoken of in this book.

Surely, we're not capable of doing that on our own but the approach, the exertion, is what allows the Surrounding Light to influence us. This means, to the extent we desire to be acquainted with the things we read, they seem to radiate their frequency onto us since all of reality is nothing other than frequencies.

Every object and each discernment has a certain frequency. When I try to acquaint myself with them, I get a certain "frequency" in response, called "Surrounding Light" and senses begin to awaken in me. Since those senses exist in me, the "*Reshimo*" exists and I only need to force myself to draw near to that first image which is within me but not yet in my consciousness. I need to force myself back into consciousness.

Excerpt from daily Kabbalah lesson, December 24, 2009

Being Impacted by *The Zohar* Like a Baby

Nature has set up a very strange entrance for man into this world. When he's born, no one explains anything to him upfront. He isn't told who his mother and father are nor given the emotions nor intellect acquired by previous generations.

He's born as "a piece of flesh" and later, begins to have impressions of this world such as heat, cold, darkness, light, sounds, noise, and silence. In the very beginning, he feels nothing and responds to nothing. Only after several weeks, we notice that he suddenly responds differently to various things. He starts responding to his mother and to things that are done with him. He starts crying, laughing, and becoming aware of the world. Suddenly, he has an internal drive to know his surroundings and his body. That's how he grows. It's a true wonder.

On the other hand, an animal is familiar with his world within the first few weeks. After a few days, he can already get along in the world to a certain extent. That's quite different to man who's not capable of doing anything without help physically from the outside. If we were to leave him in the forest, he would grow up like a beast by adapting to his habitat.

All of man's growth in our world results from impressions, examples, behavior patterns, and forms existing in our world. We create forms and games for children to take apart and put together. We use colors, sounds, and everything possible. It's all in order to develop a person so he'll be ready to go out into our world. Instinctively, we're built so that we wish to give children everything we have because, otherwise, he won't be fit for life. That's a desire that arises in us naturally and we can't influence it in any way.

It's impossible to "plug man in" to a certain computer and load him with an array of knowledge without him gradually going through the necessary stages. We can't develop senses, responses or sensitivities other than in a gradual fashion through various impressions. It usually takes approximately twenty years or even more. Actually, even we, the adults, are still learning. We're disappointed by not sufficiently knowing our world. Suddenly, at the age of 40, 50, or 60, we start thinking, "If I had only known this before…" Man continues to develop throughout his entire life.

The same applies in spirituality except that, in spirituality, one needs to discover where his mother and father and his surroundings are. Where are the forms, the games, sounds, and colors, necessary for his growth? If he doesn't receive them, he won't be fit to emerge into the spiritual world; it won't open for him and he won't recognize it.

Imagine leaving a newborn as is without investing in him but only sustaining him and no more. What would become of him? He would remain "a piece of meat." It's the same with us. If we don't receive constant, new, and different impressions from the outside, even when we don't understand them similarly to a baby who doesn't understand what's happening around him, we won't be able to grow. In spirituality, we must fill ourselves with various influences from the outside although these are truly external impressions from the spiritual world exterior to us. That influence is provided to us by *The Book of Zohar*.

Hence, it's such a unique book. No other book affects people like *The Book of Zohar*. A person who reads and hears can understand a little more, a little less, or not at all. It makes no difference. This book fills him with all kinds of impressions and influences of which he, himself, is unaware. However, gradually, similarly to the period it takes for us to grow up, we study *The Zohar* and receive constant impressions from it. Those impressions will permeate us and they, themselves, take care of our advancement.

Of course, we will be accompanying the reading of *The Book of Zohar* with certain explanations in order to allow people to connect with it to a certain extent.

Still, the truth is that one will advance even if a person reads this book without our explanation and, rather, only with his desire like a baby opening his eyes wide, instantly wanting it all, and running around since nature doesn't allow him to stay motionless for a moment. If we open our senses, our heart, and our mind to perceive that which comes from this book just like a baby looking at the world with huge eyes, we will advance.

Excerpt from the daily Kabbalah lesson, November 23, 2009

Yearning "to Understand What Is Being Taught"

The Book of Zohar is divided into different portions and some of which seem to be very "dry." Some portions are written in the language of Kabbalah, others in the language of the Bible, and still others in the language of *Halacha* (Jewish law) which discuss various holidays and the like.

However, we need not pay attention to the words themselves. It doesn't matter to me what the word is that I hear since the Kabbalists took these words from this world. The world itself seems to have nothing to do with what they would like to convey to me. What's important to me is only to receive a sort of "inner pinch" or a sensation instead of the word.

Baal HaSulam writes in "The Preface to the *Talmud Esser HaSefirot*," letter 255, that we should approach the scriptures "with a strong desire and urge to understand what is studied." 'Understanding' means to be excited, inspired, and connected. As it's written, "And Adam knew Eve his wife," which means to have an internal connection since it's from that desire that we draw the Surrounding Light. In other words, knowledge means nothing; it's only the desire that's meaningful.

Therefore, it's of utmost importance to me to desire a feeling of what's happening here rather than understanding these words because it's not possible to acquire the spiritual world with the intellect. We need new vessels developed only through our desire which draw the Light that Reforms or the "Surrounding Light."

Surely these words don't evoke particular inspiration as they are very dry. However, if despite these dry words, I search for the emotion and the image that should be depicted within me or in my desire, this gives me even greater benefit than if I read and am impressed with other expressions or those written in a different language such as that of the Bible, *Halachah,* or legends, for example. Even though the language of Kabbalah is "dry," it's actually the language which evokes a greater deficiency in us for spiritual advancement.

Excerpt from the daily Kabbalah lesson, November 25, 2009

Perceiving Reality Like a Baby

Question: What should I desire to feel when I read about "Elijah," or "Noah," for example?

Imagine you're a baby about to be born except that, in addition to the "clothing" of a baby, you will also have the understanding of a mature adult from the previous incarnation. How would you accept the world? How would you open it? Imagine what you would feel as an infant.

In other words, you exist and your exterior exists, and both of those matters are different; they are two separate worlds. How do you now reveal the world? You know nothing but you try to absorb it. You have no reference for each and every object. It can be compared to the Native Americans who didn't perceive Columbus's ships when they approached America's beaches since they had no patterns of those ships. You simply want to perceive, understand, and become familiar with the world in some way.

Excerpt from daily Kabbalah lesson, November 28, 2009

Aiming Myself toward the Goal with the Words

The possibility of being able to change ourselves by reading a certain book is truly amazing in the way it allows us to feel as if we're in a world which, at that moment, can't be felt or even imagined. With every slight change happening within us here, even if it's one millimeter toward that world, it already brings about so many huge changes like ascents, descents and all sorts of changes that we can't even comprehend.

Suddenly we're hazy. Suddenly, we find ourselves in the darkness and in different moods. You suddenly feel tall or suddenly you feel short. However, these still aren't spiritual changes but rather are psychological ones resulting from us becoming more sensitive to the occurrences in our world. The true question arises here as to how that can be. Where is that force, that "device," that causes such a great shift that I can't even explain? Certainly, the language of *The Zohar* is so unique that I constantly search for ways to explain how it works.

We have an unidentifiable goal which is a separate and concealed world so distant and opposite to us that we have no contact with it and no possibility of identifying it. However, we can aim ourselves toward it if we have two things along the way. Similar to using a rifle, we have, firstly, a scope and, secondly, an intent which we use to aim at the target and we will definitely hit it. How can that be done with *The Book of Zohar*? Instead of a scope, we have a heart and a point in the heart, and we have a mind which is undoubtedly connected to the heart supplying it with all its needs. Likewise, we have our five senses.

In order to aim ourselves toward our goal, we need to understand that *The Zohar* describes various images in the language of "*Midrash*" such as, "Every first born of an ass you shall redeem with a lamb." It uses terms such as "lamb", "mule", "ox", "cow", "Holy Temple", "sacrifices", *"Tefilin* of the arm*", and "Tefilin* of the head*"* along with all sorts of terms from the language of the "*Midrash*" that depict a corporeal image for us, meaning objects, actions and various things from this world. I should expect that at a certain moment while reading *The Book of Zohar*, I will begin to sense the desires and qualities behind all of the familiar terms from this corporeal world.

This is not about spiritual concepts like "in order to bestow", "intent to bestow", "Creator", or something from some unknown world, rather it's about my qualities to the extent that I'm capable of depicting them. In other words, I exist and behind every word, two things exist which are the physical image from this world and the desires from the spiritual world. If I'm capable of depicting these two concepts within me, if I am able to detect that behind every word there is a desire which increases, decreases, does something, or connects with something, I begin to ascribe emotions to them because the emotions are desires. I begin to notice how they exist within me and play with me. They begin to live within me and that's already something great. It's a sign that I'm aimed toward the goal. That means that my other scope is aimed at the goal and, even though I can't yet see the goal, I still aim for it.

Excerpt from the evening lesson "Zohar for All", January 30, 2010

Ascending from the Branches to the Roots

Question: Why do we need to understand the spiritual interpretation of every word of *The Zohar* rather than its simple, physical explanation?

The *Torah* shouldn't be lowered to this world. We need to ascend from the branches to the roots or from this world upward. We shouldn't take the spiritual world and lower it to our world. In any case, we don't have the same rules in our world. What would we gain by that? We would gain nothing more than unproductive imagination.

All of the confusion in our reality stems from people not understanding spirituality and not being in it. They imagine what spirituality is and then clothe it in corporeal forces. For example, it would be as if I have the force of giving in my right hand or the force of receiving in my left hand or that my body has some parts which are more sacred than others.

All of those things are absolutely unacceptable. We mustn't connect anything spiritual to things we understand and feel in our reality in this world. There is nothing sacred in our world. There's nothing sacred in the still, vegetative, animate, speaking, or in anything carried out in our world. *The Book of Zohar* is considered "holy" because it's the means through which I can ascend into holiness. "I," meaning the point in the heart, belongs to the spiritual world or the holy world and it resides within me. Contrary to my entire nature, one little point exists within me and through that means I can ascend to the holy world or to bestowal.

Still, it's not the paper or the print which are considered holy. The letters in the book aren't holy. "Holy" is the unity between the Light and the vessel which is symbolized by that letter.

Excerpt from the daily Kabbalah lesson, December 28, 2009

The World Resides Within Me

When I approach reading *The Zohar*, I must do that out of unity with the entire world or all of reality. Everything is within me. There is nothing other than me and other than the Creator.

How can I include them all within me? I can include them only if I sense them as my own: "As my own" means by love of them. However, even without using the term "love," I must approach the text from my point which is from the realization that man is a small world and the entire world is within me.

I stand before the Upper Light or before the Creator with all of the qualities and observations and with all that I have. I don't imagine anything outside me. I have no history, no geography and no universe. There is nothing other than me, the Creator, and the screen existing between us which is the relationship that I need to build with Him.

Excerpt from the daily Kabbalah lesson, December 15, 2009

Viewing Reality Correctly

If I take all of the forms and explanations that I learned in school regarding the Bible, Jacob, Esau, Issac, Abraham and everything told in *The Zohar* and approach the studying of *The Zohar* similarly, I enter a state of great confusion. I don't concentrate at all on what *The Zohar* is actually telling me. While reading, I need to emerge into space as if there is no Earth or as if it only appears that everything that once happened to him actually took place. I need to understand that time, motion, and place are imaginary notions existing in our mind alone and there is no such thing. I call "reality" the fact that I imagine that something existed two-thousand years ago and even go and dig and find certain bones. All of that exists within my mind and my emotions. However, I wish to elevate to the correct discernments regarding the desire with *"reshimot."* I wish to explore the desire with the *"reshimot"* and not that archaeology.

I want to view this entire world as existing within my desire and, truly that's where it exists. I must transfer to the true perception of reality and not to what I imagine. I want to view you as patterns or as figures within my desire and not only as bodies sitting here before me. I wish to see all of reality with my desire including the Creator. When that happens, it will be "*Malchut of Ein Sof*" and I am located within her. I need to condense it all into one and to accept that everything exists within one desire.

Why do I see so many figures, actions, operations, and motions dependent on time, motion, or place, physically or spiritually? It results from the Light which the Creator created in me. It gradually leads me to the true, correct feeling. If I want to perceive the correct reality, I mustn't see something and relate to it as occurring outside of my desire. From the time we were born, we have become accustomed to viewing this movie in a fashion as if something is there outside of us. However, this entire movie takes place in our desire.

We will have to conduct a "war" with ourselves time and time again and convince ourselves that everything takes place inside the desire. This approach doesn't erase reality because the desire is reality. Even when I encounter something now, it's the desire. The feeling that something is happening around me now constitutes desires as well and forces depicted as such before my eyes.

Why don't you imagine that those forms you see on the screen exist in the computer? This is because you know that there are electrical forces stabilizing that form for you. In comparison, you aren't aware of our world, because you can't see the "screen" upon which it's being filmed. Baal HaSulam says that there is a part in the back of our head with a "camera" through which we view the world as if it were outside of us. This means we also have a "screen" and all sorts of electrical forces stabilizing the image we see. It only seems like the stabilized image upon it is external.

Try digesting this somehow and gradually

understanding. Clearly, that's impossible but, to the extent we attempt to live this image through *The Zohar*, we will advance toward the truth or the true perception. We will begin to see everything as forces, qualities and the general activating force conducting all of these forces and qualities which is the Creator. That's the "revelation" we desire. That revelation takes place inside our desire according to the measure of equalization of form between it and the desire of the Creator. Gradually, step by step, we must aim ourselves toward that. The entire *Zohar* is aimed only toward that perception of reality.

Excerpt from the daily Kabbalah lesson December 21, 2009

The Effort During the Study

Trying is of Primary Importance

A person studying *The Zohar* goes through great and various changes. Firstly, he changes his focus on life which means the matters to which he pays attention to or not. Secondly, he becomes more introspective in his inner emotions; thirdly, his relationship with others changes and he makes more space for that.

A person studying *The Zohar* suddenly starts to think about the actions he reads in *The Zohar* and to view them as more internal acts than our world. Clearly, a person studying *The Zohar*, changes. *The Zohar* changes him, calms him, makes him more internal, more serious, and more goal-oriented. *The Zohar*'s influence is very strong and is not at all dependent on the extent of his comprehension; rather on his exertion or the extent to which he tries to perceive what is taking place here and what's being discussed.

Excerpt from daily Kabbalah lesson, December 27, 2009

The Reward is in accordance with the Effort

The Book of Zohar deliberately leaves us room for exertion, room for attempting to understand and to feel: "What is this? What for? Where is it within me?" Since all it describes takes place within each and every individual.

Even now I am performing these acts that are spoken of in *The Book of Zohar*, since I am now in the world of Infinity as well. However, there are 125 degrees of concealment of my true state between my present feeling and the world of Infinity. In order to return to the feeling of the World of Infinity, such a story is deliberately presented to me, so I will try to find within me everything that's told therein. That searching actually bears new qualities, vessels of perception and inner discernments within me, through which I begin to feel what I can't feel now. Otherwise, I won't develop the spiritual sense. That's why I need to exert myself, as it's written: "According to the exertion is one's reward." And when will I find it?! When the Upper Light influences me sufficiently, to the extent of my efforts, and fills that sense. That's how it takes place each time while ascending from one degree to the next. And the main thing is to ascend to the first spiritual degree.

Excerpt from the daily Kabbalah lesson, January 26, 2010

The Correct Effort while Studying
The Zohar

All of our focus, our entire search, is always within. Actually it happens unconsciously – even when we use the spoken language, slang, we say, "He's a scattered person, whereas he is more extroverted, more introverted, more focused," etc. It's because we sense that's how things operate in nature.

Each one of us has to search the more internal state. Actually, we will never be able to detect a higher state than the internal one adjacent to us. I may imagine, fantasize the "World of *Ein Sof*," but eventually I will discover that it's the one right next to me, slightly above my current state.

Therefore all the forces I draw together and all of my efforts should focus on detecting vessels and discernments representing every word written here:

"town", "tower", "ascending", "descending", "angels", "demons", "ghosts", "sons of Ephraim", "Yechezkel", and "the Creator descending to see what people have done."

Those things exist within me, the Upper presents this book to me, it tells me only of matters that suit me, similar to the way in which adults tell the young child about the world. We won't be capable of hearing or seeing any more than that, although this book holds much more than we see now.

It can be said that we're in the hands of a great expert on education, who knows how to present us only with what is good for us and no more. Hence, we must exert ourselves with all our strength in order to locate the discernments of the text within us. Then we rise to those discernments, we will locate them, we will live amongst them like a baby who grows in a day or two, or perhaps even in a week or a month, and is already at a new degree. He already understands, has more of an orientation, revealing deeper, internal matters, those he didn't see or recognize previously.

That's how we are. In the same text we will discover new discernments, new connections, since everything is measured by those who receive it. That's all of our work. Nonetheless, this process will lead us to the revelation that the entire world is within us, therefore, the friends' impact on us must also manifest in the common thought of attaining this internality and discovering it. When we detect that internality, we reveal that we're situated there together, that all of us comprise this image. Each and every one discovers everyone there, inside.

At a certain stage, all of these forces, all of the qualities, all of the discernments will accumulate, and there will be no conflict between them whatsoever. That's the work. Hence, it makes no difference how much we understand, rather it's the effort.

Excerpt from the daily Kabbalah lesson, December 16, 2009

Opening *The Zohar*

I am telling you from experience that while reading *The Book of Zohar*, only exercises help, more and more exercises. It's not just an obtuse book, since if we actually succeed in "unblocking" it, we can enter through it, like through a locked gate, into spirituality. However, it can happen only if I want to sense my inner world in the entire text.

In that way, time and time again, day after day, without even knowing how, all of a sudden, we will advance to a situation in which we will begin to sense something. Suddenly, after every single word we will feel inner reactions. Thus, similar to a baby discovering the world, instinctively and naturally, we will suddenly feel that a certain reality, a new world is suddenly depicted.

Excerpt from the daily Kabbalah lesson, November 25, 2009

Focusing on Reality

Try to penetrate the heart, with all of its thick layers within, and try to detect what is taking place in these layers because something is happening; only we do not feel it. *The Zohar* is situated there, the Creator is there, and the entire world—everything exists there inside, within the heart, within our desire, except I am not conscious of that and I can't detect it. I am simply sealed, as if intoxicated, unconscious of what is truly happening within me. After all, we're in the World of Infinity and everything exists. The only thing we need to do is to try harder to enter inside, probe and scrutinize where each and every thing is situated therein.

It can be described differently: Let's say we have a camera through which we should see the reality inside us. I have to change my qualities with this camera, "focus" with the lens, and perhaps with all sorts of other actions, in order for the things *The Zohar* tells me to "come into my focus," and then I will be able to see. Right now, everything is blurred and I can hardly see anything at all. Consequently, I look inside myself and see which qualities I need to alter in order to become closer to that, for it to enter my focus, and for me to see those things with my inner camera.

Simply try, no matter from which direction we approach the issue, rather only the effort of searching the inner image is essential: What am I lacking in order for it to happen? Where exactly in this image does the whole of reality exist; I, all of the other souls, the Creator, all of us together along with the revelation of our unity?

Excerpt from the daily Kabbalah lesson, November 27, 20009

Making the Effort to Merge with *The Zohar*

Question: While preparing for our lesson, we read a section which said that even if an individual doesn't understand anything in *The Zohar*, he still gains something?…

It's incorrect that we do not need to understand anything, and that even a person who doesn't understand gains something. A person gains, according to his effort to be included in what *The Zohar* says. It doesn't matter if those are good things or bad things, rather the importance is in passing through and experiencing them like an adventure. He should desire to flow with these waves *The Zohar* brings, just like with an adventure book. He should live it, be inspired, feel, cry, laugh – everything; that's what he should desire. For a start, one needs no more than that, and the mind will follow later on.

Excerpt from the evening lesson" Zohar for All ,"November2009 ,28

The Feeling of "One Man with One Heart"

The Zohar is disclosure. However this disclosure can only be within the will to bestow when he has some kind of equivalence with the Light, since the Light appears according to a quality similar to it. Meaning, to the extent one has the intent to bestow, to that extent the book will open before him. However, to the extent one is not, the book will remain blocked, secret, hidden.

Thus, in order to direct ourselves correctly, rather than out of the illusion that "I would like to bestow unto all, may they all come forth, I am ready," the best and most realistic thing to do is to make an effort to think that we're in one desire that includes within it all the points in our heart, all of our desires for spirituality. People sitting anywhere around the world watching us right now, or here, watching tv—we all exist in one desire and cancel all the other desires, except for this desire to slightly rise above our world, to unite and to feel "as one man in one heart," and to some extent discover the Upper One. This intention should be constant, and we need to keep it at least during the study.

In addition, we should remember that *The Zohar* only speaks about a person and what takes place within each and every one of us. It speaks about me, who wants to discover spirituality, is comprised of everyone, and that there is nothing else outside of me. The entire world is within me, all of the observations are within me, everything stated here – "wicked", "righteous", "Rabbi Shimon", "Rabbi Haiya", *"Malchut"*, *"Zeir Anpin"*, "Father and Mother", "souls", "worlds" – everything is inside me, just as we learned regarding the perception of reality. There is nothing else.

So when I hear a certain word, I should think that there is nothing in the world right now, I am in a space with nothing in it, including the Creator. All is within me whereas outside of me there is nothing. The entire book we're now reading explains the "topography" to me, meaning my inner structure and what is taking place within me.

Excerpt form the daily Kabbalah lesson, November 30, 2009

Everything Exists – Only Your Efforts Are Needed

The *"Torah"* speaks only of a person's internality, of the spiritual world existing within me. Desires to bestow, instead of the will to receive, constitute the "spiritual world."

At the moment, I perceive all of reality, everything included in my sensations and emotions, within me – and that's what is called "this world," since I receive it through absorption. Similarly, if I invert myself from receiving through absorption to receiving by bestowing, I will reveal the spiritual world. So I need to be entirely focused within, in order to detect these discernments within me.

You ask, why did they confuse us, the sages of *The Zohar*, Moses, who wrote the *"Torah"*, the authors of the *"Mishnah"* and *"Gemarrah"* who wrote statements such as: "The bull fighting the cow", along with all sorts of concepts; "seeds", "women", "slaves" etc, what for? One tells us of *"Sephirot"* and "worlds", the other tells about this world, about the labor of agriculture and the Holy Temple, whereas Moses tells us about a certain history. Why do they tell us about what is taking place within us, in this fashion?

You do not yet understand, but trust them that by deliberately confusing you in that fashion, they are able to direct you to enter the feeling of perception through bestowal. There is no world, no history or "worlds." Everything is in your will to receive. However in order to lead that will to receive from receiving inside itself to using it to bestow by that means, we must accept these images in this particular way. We need to make the effort to shift from this perception to another one. This effort leads us to something completely different.

Why? You do not know. Yet, just understand that there is nothing artificial here. Rather, the images

Moses expressed, or the sages of the "*Mishnah*" and the "*Talmud*" or Kabbalists or those who wrote in the language of the legends, are images describing the Light and the vessel within us. There is nothing artificial here, as if someone were to suddenly write something, rather it happens naturally.

Hence, after you hear it once, accept it and be sure of one thing only: You need to feel internally that it speaks of you alone. Ask yourself: How does that happen? Which of my qualities, desires and thoughts do I label with all of these names; "water", "flood", "Creator", "creature", "Noah", "wicked", "righteous", "sons of Noah", all kinds of "animals", "the ark", "the sky" and "earth"? It makes no difference. Every word, even each letter and element comprising that letter, each and every part, is actually a particular discernment within me. Who am I? I do not know that either. There is nothing other than one thing only – making an effort toward describing myself as comprised of all that's written here.

Just like a baby who doesn't know the language, is not familiar with or understands these words and who doesn't comprehend why each and every letter is written such and not otherwise, so too do I wish to discover everything from zero right now. And then, when I discover everything from zero, I reveal myself and the world and all that's within it, and that's what is called "I saw a reversed world." Nothing resembles anything I know now.

Excerpt from the daily Kabbalah lesson, November 30, 2009

A Person is A Small World

Question: What is that special place toward which *The Book of Zohar* directs us?

The Zohar directs us only to open the world within us, where there are all of the types of discernments: I, the world, the still, vegetative, animate, speaking and actually anything I can imagine, including myself. All of that's inside, within me. That's how I should relate to myself and *The Book of Zohar* which opens me to me. *The Zohar* tells me about myself, through all of the historical and geographic observations I read in it. All of it takes place within me.

What does it mean "takes place within me?" "I" in fact, am the "screen," and the force called the force to receive is what paints all kinds of forms, characters and actions on "my screen." This force paints still nature, the vegetative world, the animal world and the speaking world to me, on the corresponding degrees of my will to receive. All of that's portrayed within my desire, by the means of my will to receive.

Baal HaSulam explains that within us there is a type of "photographic device" which paints a pseudo-reality before us. However, the fact is that there is no reality, rather our will to receive acquires these impressions from the force residing and operating within it, which paints forms that we discern as still, vegetative, animate and human.

So, when I read *The Book of Zohar*, I have to picture me as a small world, where everything is inside me – the sea, mountains, colors, sounds, trees, people, and everything taking place happens within me. Then, I gradually begin to shift from the shapes *The Zohar* describes to properties, qualities. Instead of reading names and imagining animals, peoples, trees and everything happening with them, I gradually shift to qualities, properties. They are only divided into two qualities – bestowal and reception – at different intensities and in all kinds of ways. This is how we should try to imagine these concepts.

As soon as I actually transcend into the world of the forces, I begin to see the truth: All of the forms I see now are an "imaginary world," whereas really they are all forces, behind which I gradually identify One Force. That's how we should read *The Zohar.*

Excerpt from the daily Kabbalah lesson ,December2009 ,9

"I Labored and I Found"

Question : How does reading *The Zohar* affect a person's emotions when he has just begun his spiritual path?

For now it's psychology: We read and attempt to enter the text. A person entering the study is confused and incapable of finding himself internally. It's not in vain that it's written, "I labored and I found." You have the object of your labor, internal labor, rather than merely reading or hearing, but to constantly labor in the attempt to connect this picture and invert it to the true one as much as possible. It doesn't matter that you get confused at every given moment, run away from it and return once more. That's actually good. But this effort, of significantly trying to construct your internal world correctly at every moment is called "I have labored," and later, "I have found" will follow, when you discover that which stands before you.

Excerpt from the daily Kabbalah lesson, December 10, 2009

The Work of the Lord

While studying, a person should crave to know where he is, who he is, how he connects with the Creator, and how he reveals all of his qualities. Within them he discovers: "That's me, reality, the system and that's how I connect with the Creator. The entire world is inside me, and all that I discover is all of the souls."

The Zohar speaks exactly of this inner work. He provides us with what is called "The field that was blessed by the Creator." By reading and searching for all of those qualities and forces within him, *The Zohar* enables a person to find the components of the soul, the extent to which he is capable of being in these qualities or not, and what he is lacking in order to be in each and every one of them. The states a person goes through, probes and discerns – that's the true work of the Creator.

Excerpt form the daily Kabbalah lesson, December 15, 2009

Trying to Build the Connection with the Creator

It's not so important what we understand or not while reading *The Book of Zohar*. Questions can be asked, if you wish, but the main thing is to try. We should try to understand what they want to tell us, as much as possible.

They aren't telling us about history, geography or the stars, rather only about correcting the soul. All of the wisdom of Kabbalah speaks only about the correction of the soul, about the way I achieve the connection with the Creator. According to what we learned, all that exists are Light, the vessel and the screen between them. The Creator relates to the person, and the person has to relate back to the Creator. If he can relate to Him correctly, corresponding to the way the Creator relates to him, he reveals the Creator and their connection.

The Zohar tells us about the way to build this connection between us, and the other details we read are insignificant. That's because *The Zohar* speaks only about the way I open my soul, thus feeling and connecting in contact with the Creator.

Excerpt form the daily Kabbalah lesson, December 25, 2009

Searching for *The Zohar* Within Me

The Zohar speaks of the internal scrutiny I must conduct within. Not a single word here is about this world, but only about a person's inner world. Man is a small world.

I must delve within me and find which of my qualities reflect each word written here. There are only two qualities within me: reception and bestowal, nothing more.

Start digging inside and search, as if in the dark with the light of a candle, where those two qualities reside within you, the way *The Zohar* refers to them.

And then within you, a new space with a vast array of qualities of reception and bestowal will begin to be revealed, and all the words of *The Book of Zohar* will find their place therein.

Like a child who gradually learns to sense the world around him, so a new internal world will be created within you. Then you will realize that even this world, to which you are accustomed, is sensed within you.

In this manner *The Book of Zohar* changes you. But this happens only if we search within for all that's being read, without trying to judge everything intellectually, as something external to us.

Excerpt from the daily Kabbalah lesson, Nov 20, 2009

Returning to Consciousness

I have desire, and nothing else exists. Within this desire, there is something, let's say, called "David", "Abraham", "Isaac", "Moses", "Joseph", "right", "left", "middle", "Hell", "Garden of Eden", etc. All sorts of things and all within the desire. It's impossible for me to feel, depict or think about anything which is not the desire. The Creator created only desire. Now, I have to begin to know my desire. I live within it, but I do not know how I exist. I activate it, it activates me. That's considered being "unconscious."

The Zohar begins to revert us to a state of consciousness. It begins to explain to me the components of my desire, how to bestow, how I arrange them, correct them, update them. Thus, for example, I am incapable of working with my main desire called "David", *"Malchut"*. I have to receive corrections from "Abraham", "Isaac", etc. into that desire. In the meantime I only hear, but I want to know it. It's all my desire, it's within me.

If I want to know this desire, yearning for it like a baby, the Surrounding Light reaches me from a clearer state and shines toward me, and I begin to slightly sense that state. I begin to ascribe a feeling to each such discernment – one is not so pleasant, another is slightly more pleasant, one is lower, one is higher. That's how I advance because we have nothing other than the feeling.

Excerpt from the daily Kabbalah lesson, December 21, 2009

Seeing the True Reality

When we sit with *The Zohar*, we read about the elements existing in our spiritual vessel. What is "the spiritual vessel?" It depends on my attitude. There is no corporeal vessel or spiritual vessel rather it depends on the person. The spiritual vessel is revealed when I begin to approach myself and the entire world as one desire created by the Creator, which I only sense as thousands of desires, different qualities, moving in separate directions and for varied purposes – each is different, all is shattered and scattered in every direction. From a state of not seeing the cause of what is happening and where it all is going, I have to begin to approach it as one single entity, as one vessel, for everything I see is my soul.

I have to assemble all of these data realistically to the best of my ability, not in an imaginary way, and to scrutinize my attitude toward everything that happens.

In the meantime I do nothing, enabling the Light to operate. As written: "There is nothing new under the sun." I relate to everything as always and request the Light to scrutinize the correct picture called "world" for me, these desires – whether they are mine or not, whether they are inside or outside of me. I am still confused. But gradually by studying I draw the Light, try to be with everyone, think that we're one vessel, and through that I begin to see the correct reality.

It can be resembled to a newborn baby beginning to sense reality – he doesn't know where he is headed or what he is about to feel. Similarly, we also do not know and do not need to know where we're going. It will be revealed. How? It doesn't matter to me. Kabbalists only provide us with certain simple rules – "You should crave" – and if we do crave, we won't have to do anything further. Our action is only to open ourselves as much as possible to the direction from which our new order should arrive.

Excerpt form the daily Kabbalah lesson, December 23, 2009

The Way to Enter the Feeling of the Spiritual World

I am teaching you how to "focus" on the spiritual world. To the extent you develop eyes for it, you will be able to see it and then you will understand and feel. It's written "We can only judge what we see" and "If we do not attain, we won't know." What will you gain by knowing names if you haven't attained them? Therefore we're now learning how to attain these concepts. "Attainment" means that it's clear to me through all my senses and intellect; I am in that state, I live it, am immersed in and comprised of it, it is I.

We're speaking of the way we enter that feeling. Similar to the way an infant enters this world, naturally and simply. Can we give intellectual reasoning? What can we explain to him? First, he must be filled with all kinds of impressions. Afterwards, he attains various observations: This is hot, that's cold, this is light, that's dark, this is hard, that's soft, etc. As a result he begets intellect, which teaches him that this is good for him and that's bad for him. He is drawn to this but not to that. However, all of that's only after he reveals those observations. Similarly, we're now about to reveal the spiritual reality, and that's what we're discussing. Hence, there is no point asking me "What is that on the inside?" because it's not up for discussion. I want us to learn only about the way to enter such a feeling. We have to take the way we view this world and deliberately "break the focus." Not to see this world, rather to focus on an entirely other spot, to focus on it attentively and begin to see through it alone. It resembles 3-D pictures, for when you look at them, at first you do not see anything. However, when we do not look at the picture's surface, when our focus is spread out instead of focused on the picture itself, rather attempting to somewhat enter it, we begin to see. That's the type of effort we're speaking about during the study of *The Zohar*.

Excerpt from the daily Kabbalah lesson, December 23, 2009

Yearning Is the Prayer

Prior to every portion we read from *The Zohar*, we have to return to the intention. We're now dealing with the internal Torah, revealed within a person. We have all kinds of thoughts, later all kinds of desires are awakened in us, and we also have all kinds of qualities; and within their core, the spiritual reality we're reading about is revealed. Hence, all of our concentration and anticipation should focus on revealing this reality inside, within us.

I should constantly tend to that, to try to see where and how I respond to it: Is anything within me shifting in correspondence with these words? Even imagine it, it doesn't matter. Try to locate these internal motions, and the yearning itself already constitutes prayer. After we become accustomed to approaching the text in this way, we will add our interconnection to the habit, since *The Zohar* was written only in order to build that connection.

And even this interconnection, is not amongst the bodies, rather inside, within us. Within me, all of the points of all of the souls exist, each and every one, and I have to construct that connection within, between what is called the "I" and the image, the model of all the rest of the souls. Within that connection I build my internal spiritual vessel, within which Divinity will be revealed. In other words, all concentration should be internal.

It makes no difference which words we read. We can read words that remind us of names or places from the Bible, or all kinds of plants and animals, or work in the Holy Temple, or all sorts of human actions, such as love, hate, birth, or death. It makes no difference. We have to constantly remember that they all refer only to my internal phenomena.

I do not hear the word itself, rather wish to locate what is behind it, the response I should have toward it, and only then do I understand the meaning of the word. It is so, because the words themselves have been taken from this world, but they should lead me to an inner sensation of the internal world, the Upper world.

Excerpt from the daily Kabbalah lesson, November 25, 2009

Hardships as Blessings

We should relate to *The Zohar* as a remedy. What I read is not important, whereas the searching itself is, the desire to locate in me all that's happening internally. There are times when a person succeeds in that and he "flourishes," reacting internally to every word, and sometimes he doesn't. However, we have to understand that if we say that primarily during the study of *The Zohar*, it is the effort put forth, so actually, the difficult times when I exert myself yet find nothing in the text, but force myself to continue, those are the most useful times for my advancement; much more than other times, in which I seem to be able to find a positive reaction for every word in the text, discover discernments within me and am inspired. In short, "The opinion of "Torah" is opposite of the opinion of the landlords," as Rabash, my teacher used to say.

In fact, in situations when it's difficult for us to

penetrate the text, we achieve a great deal from every tiny effort, compared to situations in which you are inspired and do not exert yourself, rather allow yourself to go with the flow, and thus lose out. In other words, particularly the times when a person hangs on with his teeth are the most efficient. Those

are the conditions for actual work, in which we have to try to concentrate ourselves inward, further and further and to locate that particular word or concept within us, that combination of them, etc. By these efforts, we grow, like a baby.

Sometimes, when I work on texts, it takes me three or four hours to enter the text and see something. I know nothing can be done, other than the exertion that must be made and the time that needs to pass. Actually, those hours when I anticipate entering it are the best hours for advancement.

Hence, you should view those situations as a blessing – you are being given space for work, the opportunity to gain, and you are being told that now is the time to exert yourself. Bring your strength, focus yourselves, try and you will succeed. So let's not miss those things and "open" ourselves, search inside us for all the discernments of which *The Zohar* speaks.

Excerpt from the daily Kabbalah lesson, December 20, 2009

Yearning for Sanctity in the Dark

When I read *The Book of Zohar*, I should yearn to sense that it speaks of me. It tells me in a very strange way, somewhat weird, what is happening inside of me, and me alone. I have a liver, lungs, kidneys, spleen, digestive system, etc. Besides those systems, I also have emotions and that alone is spoken about in this book. Within that feeling there are many desires, qualities, thoughts, urges of sorts. I have to ask myself: Other than my flesh, who is the human being inside me and what do I see? Exactly what the authors of *The Zohar* describe here to us. Within this "person" inside me, there are qualities called "Jacob", "Esau", "ox" "ass", "birds", "trees", "Adam", and "Noah's ark." "Tree" is a very special desire in me, a unique quality. The "ark" is a special quality within which I can hide and be protected.

I have to start working with that. What does it give

me? In truth, it doesn't give me anything, nothing at all. However, by trying to locate these things, a force called "The Light that Reforms" reaches you, and for it you should yearn. Let's say you leave the lesson and say to yourself: "I succeeded! Today I felt I understood who Jacob, Esau, Israel and others are." Well, so what? It means nothing. It's possible that the next time you leave, you will say to yourself: "I didn't understand anything, everything is dry, I couldn't concentrate. I managed to make an effort to detect it inside me for only a few minutes." Yet, those few minutes are your profit.

That's "concealment." Only one who invests himself, respecting these times when there is the sensation of tastelessness and a lack of enlightenment, and yet he still wants to advance toward bestowal, he alone profits.

It's not in vain that Baal HaSulam writes in the "The Preface to the Talmud Esser HaSefirot" that the states of concealment are actually the ones in which you can exert yourself, and show that you truly long to be near the Creator. It's undoubtedly completely opposite to everything we're accustomed to in this world where we judge everything according to our egoistic feeling.

Hence, whoever works in the dark and feels it's pointless, needs to understand that these situations are very useful for advancement toward bestowal, to such an extent that with time, he won't wish for other states, rather will realize that the effort is the reward. Those moments in which you are being given the opportunity to exert yourself, without receiving anything that revives your ego, your evil inclination, your pride, understanding, intellect, or feeling – yet you still have the opportunity to strain a little and make immense efforts – those are the best situations. The ability to reach such a point of contact with Sanctity in the darkness constitutes the reward. During those states, you are clearly not being bribed by your will to receive.

Accordingly, we should be happy with pointless states.

They are the means for a person's growth. Surely, the support of the society and the general inspiration and excitement are vital, including our friends all around the world. When you do not receive support from the Creator (although it does appear from Him) you can long for the support of the group, and that's best. A public prayer is appropriate here, for true, correct effort.

Excerpt from the daily Kabbalah lesson, December 20, 2009

Persistence and Exertion in the Right Direction

Question: What is more important while studying _The Book of Zohar_: Persistence, exertion or intellectual preparation?

Only exertion and persistence are necessary, without any intellect. In "The Preface to the Talmud Esser HaSefirot", letter 133, it describes the way a person attempts to climb a mountain as all the king's guards consistently stop him. He has to pass those guards, be wiser, more persistent, and stronger. He has to overcome all of those hardships and somehow get up this mountain, thus being worthy of reaching the king.

Surely physical fitness is not the issue here, wisdom or cleverness. Patience is all that's needed. However, it's important to correctly choose exertion in the right direction – a group that assists you in directing yourself. That's all that's needed – persistence in revealing the goal and patience in its attainment. I tell you this out of my own experience and that of many of my students.

Excerpt from the virtual lesson on *The Book of Zohar*, December 27, 2009

Confusion and Disturbances while Studying

Constructing the Correct Approach to Life

Yesterday, someone asked me: "How should I behave in my life when I hear that everything is inside, that everything is within me? How should I view the world? How should I view my loved ones, my enemies, and in general everything that goes on around me?" I understand that people get confused when they hear of various internal observations, but they have to understand that there is a desired situation and reality, meaning what we sense exists, and "we can only judge what we see." Hence, we have to work and have to talk.

On the other hand, we aim ourselves to attain truer vision, more internal, and independent of ego, our will to receive. We aim to disclose the concealment, to reveal the truth and to exist in a world of two forces: The force of the Creator and the force of the creature.

That's a different world from the one we live in today, where the force of the Creator is concealed and only the force of the creature is revealed. In addition, we learn that there is another reality, in which we see it all as two forces within us, with no reality outside.

However, these things aren't realistic yet. We're incapable of understanding that we're in a movie and that our lives change to the extent this movie changes. We still think something may happen with our world, since in the meantime we only see one angle of reality.

Hence, when we speak of what *The Zohar* wants to bring us, we should still try to truly enter it, even though we will return to life in our world afterwards. However, while I read *The Zohar* and am immersed in it, I have to truly be there, since I am still incapable of being in two worlds. In the meantime, I am only in my present state and therefore have to disconnect from it and try to construct the true image. This is like a child who wishes to behave as an adult and for everyone to always treat him like an adult, rather than occasionally.

That's how we should imagine it with all our senses and fantasize as much as possible, that of which *The Zohar* speaks, the new world in which we reside. Meaning, the attributes we now own and in which we view our new reality. In this reality we live within our desires – the desire of the Creator and in our desires, in two desires which are revealed as contradictory within us. We sense them and are situated between them as a third line, as "I," and outside of me nothing exists: The two forces – and the "I" situated between them.

Excerpt from the daily Kabbalah lesson, December 16, 2009

Raising the Point in the Heart Above the Disturbances

At times during the lesson, a person's thoughts regarding all kinds of corporeal problems take over, as if he must solve them at this particular time. "Corporeal" problems mean anything belonging to this world, through which we have to rise to the spiritual world.

These corporeal problems depicted before us are our tools, which, by overcoming them, we ascend. Indeed, work, the bank, the supermarket, health, children, etc. are spiritual degrees that descended into this world and stand before you with all their conflicting traits. The bank, the ATM, health, etc. are degrees through which you have to push yourself into spirituality, they are a sort of dense and tight sieve through which you must pass.

The difficult conditions the Upper degrees create for you cause you to feel the necessity for the Light that Reforms. Hence, particularly when times are difficult for a person, you should separate the point in the heart from the pile of corporeal problems and thoughts and rise above them. If a person "pulls himself together" and continues to consistently read and study *The Book of Zohar*, then the obscurity, fog and confusion dissipate.

The Light works upon us! Time will overcome what the mind can't. *The Book of Zohar* is particularly strong in that area. We only need to give it the chance to flow freely through us. We should read each section of *The Zohar*, absorb it so it may fill all our cells and all of our anticipation.

Excerpt from the daily Kabbalah lesson, December 31, 2009

Above All Confusion and Disturbances – Try Clinging to the Friends

Question: How does our reading now, during the lesson help us intermingle and attain the deficiency for the revelation of the Creator?

You should unite with all of the friends with your mind and emotion, however, primarily with the emotion and not with the intellect. Likewise, we need to do this everywhere around the world and with the entire world, since all of us – those who understand, those who do not understand, those who are conscious, or partially conscious, it makes no difference – we're all parts of *"Malchut"* of "Atzilut." There is nothing below *"Malchut"* of "Atzilut." If we correct Her, everything will turn into the world of "Atzilut," and will ascend even higher into the world of "Ein Sof."

Therefore, we must first think about us all being in the system. Secondly, we should desire to sense that system. That system is me. Everything written and spoken about takes place within me alone – "water", "wicked", "righteous", "buildings", "breakings", "destruction" – no matter what, it all speaks of me. And not only of me, but what I am built of and in that which I am included. I want to experience those parts, experience those images, those states of which *The Book of Zohar* speaks.

The Zohar provides you with the patterns: *"Malchut"* is in the form of "Divinity", "maidservant", "mistress", "destruction"; you are in a certain situation toward "Yesod", "Tifferet", toward all that's situated below the Tifferet. It constantly gives you various situations and you need only to want to sense and actually reside within them, since surely, we're all situated in all of those states, images, and layers within us. All is there; I need only to attain it, meaning to feel that picture inside me.

However, there surely is occasional haziness, sometimes of the senses and other times of the intellect. At times there's confusion with other issues. Sometimes you suddenly picture this world. It speaks of the destruction of the Holy Temple, and all of a sudden, you think of the destruction in Jerusalem. How could that be? Yet, that's what you think. You begin to think of Noah, Adam and Abraham, and about it all actually having taken place in ancient Babylon or all different kinds of such images. Sometimes you are in a state of some dullness, causing you to picture all sorts of corporeal forms.

Hence you get opportunities for exertion wherein you can begin to concentrate once more and locate spirituality as if through binoculars, until it again becomes clear to you and you enter it. Hence, by entering and exiting, you build yourself anew each time.

Thus, "It's not the wise who learn", not with intellect, rather with patience. Read a portion and another portion, a week will pass and another one, perhaps another month and then you will begin to feel how this is working upon you.

Excerpt from the evening lesson "Zohar for All", November 15, 2009

The Zohar and
Bonding with Others

The Complete Kli (Vessel) for Revealing *The Zohar*

The Zohar is not revealed unless studied in a group. It's impossible to study *The Zohar* alone because *The Zohar* was written by a group of Kabbalists who formed a complete *Kli*. All of the ten authors of *The Zohar* formed a complete *Kli*, the ten fundamental *Sefirot*. Each one of them represents a specific *Sefira*, a unique force that the Creator created as a complete *Kli*.

Therefore ,only if we long to form such a perfect *Kli* among us will we receive this message from them, and have it affect us. Otherwise, it won't happen. If we study and try to do this in any way possible, we will very quickly feel how this force, which is concealed in *The Zohar*, affects and unites us. However, we will be able to receive their message and slightly perceive it only to the extent of our unity.

"Understanding" means "The heart understands", are desires which are already set up to comprehend the spiritual message, that which they want to convey to us emotionally. It's not possible to study intellectually and if it's possible it is then the "potion of death."

Therefore, there must be a group which has been prepared, has already reached a certain point of despair as a result of the phases it went through. In that group, there must be people who thought of attaining spirituality alone and along their way, went through illusions and clarifications of all sorts. At the end of all those discernments, after they are prepared to nullify themselves to a certain extent and see that they won't attain that alone – only then it's worth approaching *The Zohar* and being included in all that's found there. For then, they will already be prepared to merge, to be annulled.

Excerpt from Kabbalah lesson, November 19, 2009

Revealing the Creator among the Souls

In order to understand *The Book of Zohar* we have to unite, to find the points of contact among us and to try to reveal our interconnection. Through this connection we will be able to open *The Zohar*, since everything it speaks of is found among the souls, among our desires.

If we desire to bestow upon each other, our desires will be called "souls." Then, in the connection among the souls, we will reveal the "Creator," the Light that ties and bonds us together. That's what *The Book of Zohar* says, it guides us how to reveal that Light. Hence, we should think of the way to achieve unity, *"Arvut"* and "Love thy neighbor as thyself," in order to reveal the Light and *The Book of Zohar* will assist us.

Excerpt from the daily Kabblah lesson, November 24, 2009

Mutual *"Arvut"* in the Study of *The Zohar*

Question: What is *"Arvut"* while studying? How can I help the friend?

"Arvut" while studying means that if the friends aren't thinking of me and I am not thinking of them, mutually, nothing will happen. It's not enough to just read *The Zohar*, since we need to approach it with the demand for correction. And correction is in unity. Hence, I want to help the others, and for the others to help me. That's why we have gathered here together. Among us we can reveal mutual bestowal, in which we will be able to feel the Creator, the force that created us, the force that sustains us, that same force we're incapable of revealing without "Arvut," as took place at the event of Mount Sinai.

Excerpt from the daily Kabbalah lesson, November 27, 2009

Unity Before All

Question: While studying, I need to connect emotionally with the text, yet on the other hand, I must also think about unity. However, if I think of unity, I distance myself from the text, whereas when I think about the text emotionally, I distance myself from the unity. How can I combine the two?

I will give you a "tip." Imagine you are amongst the Kabbalists who wrote *The Zohar*, amongst the sages of *The Zohar*. Ten people sitting in a group, all of them are great Kabbalists, and you are bonded with them in love, in unity and in everything, and you want to hear what they are saying. As if you are amongst them, invisible, like a young child. Try that if you can do nothing else, perhaps it will help. But the bond must take place. So if you aren't able to unite with the friends beside you, try doing that and you might succeed.

Excerpt from the evening lesson "Zohar for All", November 28, 2009

The Book of Zohar **Affects a Group**

We need to understand *The Book of Zohar* affects the group, not the individual person. Hence, if we do not think of the bond among us while studying, we will miss the primary issue. We have to be united while reading *The Book of Zohar*, and think only of uniting the vessels with each word and in every discussion.

You may say: "But you always say that we should sense the issues within us, that we need to enter and there, within our desires, search for the animals, the fish, Noah, the Creator, the people within us, and work with them. Whereas here, you are again reverting back to the external group."

However, the group is not external. The group is the sorting out and the putting together of all the desires within me that are called "exterior to me." Everything I feel that's outside me is actually inside me. I have to connect the concept of the "I" within me with the concept of "externality", the "others" inside me. I do not feel the others are outside my body, rather inside me, within my desires. That's how my desires are divided.

The wisdom of Kabbalah teaches us that there is internality and externality of the vessel, the surrounding and the interior, and that we should correct the internality along with the externality by uniting them. Hence the "group" represents the desires I attach to me. You may say: "Wait, what is the meaning of 'connect everyone to me?' After all I have desires which I am incapable of correcting!" Therefore I reply that you attach them, sort them out and only then say: "This, I am incapable of correcting, but it's mine, nothing exists that isn't mine."

Such an approach allows the person to include the entire world, as written: "Man is a small world." Hence, it's vital to constantly think of that and to invest even further mutual efforts in it each time. Each one of us should delve inside himself, sort out and arrange these issues within him. That's how we should conduct ourselves throughout the day, from reading to reading of *The Book of Zohar*. Only in that way will we reveal   wholeness and not be confused.

Excerpt from the daily Kabbalah lesson, December 7, 2009

The Obligation to Provide Everyone with the Power to Cling to *The Zohar*

There is the issue of *"Arvut"* (mutual consideration) while studying *The Zohar*. Hence, each one of us should be committed to the surroundings; to cling to the topic we studied with all our force, to gain impressions from it, and to sense it internally. We need for it to live in us throughout the day, and to want all of our friends to be in a continual, inner feeling of those images and pictures which *The Zohar* brings a person during the entire day.

Therefore, at work, business, home, or with the family, we should focus our attention and mind to that place to the extent to which it's necessary, whereas we should focus all the rest of our strength upon what we study and the things inspiring us in our lessons.

In this way, each one will provide the surroundings with the *"Arvut"* and the surroundings will provide him with *"Arvut,"* the necessities and the strength to cling to that inspiration, so that the Light of *The Zohar* will begin to affect us. If we do that, we will simply begin to feel things we have never felt in the past. It all depends on the necessity each one feels, along with the commitment of each one of us toward the surroundings, in true *"Arvut."* When it's so, we will rapidly succeed in that.

Excerpt from the evening lesson, "Zohar for All", November 15, 2009

Correcting the Connection between Us

In many cases, *The Zohar* writes that "all is one," and provides an explanation which connects various things. If we also intend to see things that way, we will truly begin to see how it accumulates and is revealed as one. Let's begin now, during this lesson, to do an exercise, for everything *The Zohar* describes to be happening between the others and me. It's actually true, except that at times we may search inside and at other times, outside, "out of our skin," beyond us, external to us. *The Zohar* speaks only about the connection between the others and me. "Right", "left", "middle", and all the types of relationships only speak of this connection.

Why? Because when this connection existed, there was nothing to discuss, all was revealed, the vessel and the Light were complete. However, the connection was then broken. And what do we need to do now? To correct it. Hence, all of the wisdom of Kabbalah speaks only of the way to correct the connection among us, among the souls. The "souls" denotes the will to bestow within us.

All three lines, ten *"Sephirot"*, faces, worlds, one hundred and twenty-five degrees – all of these are only in the connection between each and every one and in all, until everything is connected and complete adhesion is created.

Excerpt from the daily Kabbalah lesson, January 31, 2010

Everything is Attained through Unity

When we speak about the general reality, we surely need to connect together. *The Zohar* doesn't speak of any other form; rather everything is said in reference to *"Malchut"*, Divinity, and "Assembly of Israel." Hence, to the extent a person wants to view reality correctly, meaning through "Malchut," which is called "the picture of the Lord," he identifies with the quality of "Malchut," which includes everyone. To the extent he is prepared to be included with everything, with everyone, he attains "Love thy neighbor as yourself." How else can all be united? There is no other connection.

We will be able to sense the true reality *The Zohar* tells us about, to hear it or even see it, only if we're ready to fulfill this condition – to be included in "Malchut," which includes all within Her, to want to absorb all of those Upper qualities inside us, and thus to resemble "*Keter*" (Crown). In order to do that, we have to think about the entire world and complete correction, for all the creatures to unite into one bundle, with the intention of bringing contentment to their Maker. Among all of those creatures, we have a large group in which we all bond together, and through this study, the rest of the human pyramid is led to the same task.

It's very helpful to think about that unity, at least once in a while. That will cause us to correspond with the Surrounding Light, and then it will affect us. If we completely forget about it, if we become detached, it won't succeed.

If we're in a feeling of envy, hatred, or in a state of rejecting of unity, *The Zohar* won't help. As is written in *The Zohar* itself, the friends arrive and discover that they hate each other, but then they overcome that, until they begin to love each other. It's this particular process which is called "the preparation for the study of *The Zohar*."

We need to pay special attention to this part of the wisdom of Kabbalah. *The Zohar* speaks to all, and its goal is only to connect. The moment there is a connection, we sense what takes place within it. The spiritual world manifests in the unity, the Creator exists in the unity, and He is already there, we do not need to do anything, except attain that picture which already exists. All these degrees exist; we do not have to do build them. We only need to adapt ourselves to those degrees, and then, to the extent we're adapted to them, we will sense what is taking place within them.

Everything is attained only through the intensity of the connection – the greater the intensity of the connection, thus the revelation will be stronger and higher.

Excerpt from the daily Kabbalah lesson, November 22, 2009

Being One Vessel

Question: Does reading *The Book of Zohar* together draw the "Surrounding Light" which can greatly effect change in all of humanity?

If I identify with all those reading *The Book of Zohar* right now, I receive what everyone receives, since we're all one soul. I receive, to the extent that I am in this single soul, this single vessel. Whereas, to the extent that I disconnect and think of myself, that I am included in them in order to receive something for myself, I receive nothing.

I must be included in them, along with them, as one structure created by the Creator. The Creator created one person, and all of this division into foreign and different desires, is a figment of our imagination.

Who receives the Light arriving from the Creator? The *"Malchut," "Shechina,"* gathering all of the souls.

I merit to the extent I have merged with all these other souls in "Malchut," to the extent I bring about the coupling with *"Zeir Anpin."*

Excerpt from the daily Kabbalah lesson, December 14, 2009

"If You Aren't In *'Malchut'*, You Do Not Exist."

Question: *The Book of Zohar* evokes powerful internal experiences within me. However, as soon as I try to think of the unity among the souls, it all instantly disappears and I can no longer focus on the text I am reading. What should I do?

Imagine you are connecting with the Creator through a system called a collection of souls, *"Malchut"* from the world of *"Atzilut"*, and that otherwise you aren't able to connect with the Creator, with *"Zeir Anpin."* Your desire is to unite all the fragments of the broken souls, you want to be with them in *"Malchut"* from the world of *"Atzilut"* and unite with *"Zeir Anpin."*

If you can't imagine connecting all the souls within you and bringing them to connecting with the Creator – then you do not exist in relation to spirituality. You should try to see this image within you.

"Malchut" – it's not your desire to become filled for your own sake, rather the desire to unite with the rest of the souls that you feel are distant and separate from you. The more I want to unite with them, my existence in *"Malchut"* will be more substantial. *"Malchut"* of the world of *"Atzilut"* is a result of my efforts to unite with the other souls; it's the common desire of all the souls!

This situation resembles the event of receiving the *"Torah"* at Mount Sinai, where all of us were obligated to unite "as one man with one heart" in order to unite with the Creator. The central point in which we unite with the Creator is called *"Malchut"* of *"Atzilut."*

Excerpt from daily Kabbalah lesson, January 3, 2010

Searching for an External Force for Advancement

Through *The Book of Zohar*, the Creator shows us all kinds of examples which inspire us. We do not understand them, yet we want to copy them, like a small child. If you do not want to or are unable to, you should turn to the group or approach with a request for help from the books. You are obligated to search for something that will push you forward and help you bond with the situations and the actions that *The Book of Zohar* tells you, even though you understand nothing, and yet want to understand.

Upper states are being discussed, spiritual bestowal, and I want to feel them and to be in them! How can I do that? All these questions should constantly bother us. It doesn't matter if I don't remember anything of what I read. But if I expected the text to influence me, if I wanted to enter that world, to feel that which *The*

Zohar speaks of – then I will feel very intensely how reading it influences me, although I do not remember a single word.

My moods, my different qualities, my perspective of the world and myself, they will all change. I will begin to feel all kinds of changes daily, until one sunny day the leap will occur. All of that will happen as a result of reading *The Book of Zohar*. I do not know of what I read, and what it is that it wants to tell me. I have no connection with it other than one thing – I want this book to be revealed to me.

That's the way the Surrounding Light operates, it's a true miracle. After all, other than that miracle, there is no other influence upon us from the Upper world. This miracle operates upon us even though there is no connection between us. There is no connection between the will to receive and the will to bestow. Any connection is carried out by the Creator, who is the source of all. Hence, this concealed connection is called a "miracle" or "remedy."

Of course there are very strict rules operating here regarding the relationships between the Light and the desire, according to a precise formula of mutual actions between them, but that formula is concealed from me. Thus, for me – it's a miracle. I press a button in one place and in other place something jumps up, and I do not understand how that works. All that's said is that I should read and will, and all the rest will arrive on its own.

Excerpt from the daily Kabbalah lesson, January 28, 2010

Receiving Strength from the Surroundings to Broaden the Point in the Heart

A person who truly yearns for spirituality won't calm down and suffice with the minimum. He will constantly have the feeling that he doesn't understand or know, since he doesn't sense spirituality. The urgency to sense the Upper world is exactly what brings about the awakening of the point in the heart, the feeling that I must sense this spiritual image inside me.

The Book of Zohar: It's an adventure book! But not the type I read or watch on a movie screen. One has to enter *The Book of Zohar*, not like in our world of illusion and imagination. We have to rid ourselves of all illusions, delusions and fantasy.

The demand for that arrives from the point in the heart, and only the group is capable of increasing and enlarging it. Only a group is able to provide that extra necessary force to the point in the heart of a person in order to attain the goal. Thus, if a person doesn't nullify himself toward the group in order to receive that force from it, he will attain nothing. That's the essence of our mutual *"Arvut,"* without which none of us would attain the spiritual vessel.

Excerpt from daily Kabbalah lesson, January 28, 2010

Keeping the Friends in Thought Above All Disturbances

The Zohar doesn't only tell of spiritual qualities and acts, rather also about the tight bond among the souls. In order to feel and restore that, we have to study *The Zohar* within a group of friends who think like us.

The internal attitude we should have toward studying may be compared to the relationships among the crew on a boat caught in stormy waters. All of the team members situated on the deck hold each other, so that the stormy waves won't sweep them away.

If anyone lets go of his friend's hand and tries to hold on to the ship's railing, he is instantly drawn into the open sea.

So it is with the study of *The Book of Zohar*: We have to hold each other with the force of our common thought, in order to overcome all the disturbances on the way to spiritual bonding.

To the extent of our bond, we will be filled with the Light of "Hochmah," the Light of life and we will elevate to a state where we will dry the sea, meaning, we will absorb all of the Light of life into us and advance, as if on land, toward the safe haven, toward the World of Infinity.

Excerpt from the Virtual Zohar Lesson, December 6, 2009

Kabbalah.info

Printed in Great Britain
by Amazon